HOW TO COMPLAIN

BRUCE SILVERMAN

COMPLAIN

FOR FUN AND PROFIT

ComplainForFunAndProfit.com

www.complainforfunandprofit.com
Mario Schulzke, Publisher

Cover design by Michael Vitellaro
Cover photo by Nancy Silverman
Cartoons by Bruce Silverman
Book design by Mario Schulzke

To Nancy,
the only person who I have
never had reason to complain
about.

Introduction

Some people collect stamps. Others, coins. Still others, sea shells, wine corks or art.

My passion is *complaining*.

But...

...and this is a very important but...I do not whine. I do not cry. I do not kvetch. I do not make a total pain in the ass of myself.

I simply complain. Like a gentleman.

I write *letters*.

To airlines. Hotels. Restaurants. Retail chains. Manufacturers.

My letters invariably can be described as "praising with faint damn." And every one of my letters is intended to obtain recompense for the sins that have been inflicted upon me.

Now I have to admit that I am rarely so satisfied with *any* experience that I don't feel compelled to complain. That is, of course, the nature of a professional complainer. (It's also why a lot of my friends characterize me as "Mr. Indignity.") Experiences that most people would rate as a B+, I am compelled to react negatively to. In fact, I've actually complained when even I would grade my experience an "A."

The reason for that seeming anomaly: I do not complain merely to complain.

I complain to *get* something. A free ticket. A free room. A free meal. A free product. And I nearly always succeed.

I've often been asked, "How do you do it? Why do your letters work (almost) every time?" Until now, my answer has been, "that's my secret."

But the time has come. My methods and techniques are now yours to share. I hope you enjoy learning and using them. And if you don't… well, feel free to complain!

— Bruce "Mr. Indignity" Silverman

Who is
"Mister Indignity?"

This book is about how to write complaint letters.

If you read it and use it, you're going to make yourself feel better — and more importantly, learn how to get all sorts of stuff for free, including money.

There is nobody more qualified to write a book about how to complain than Bruce "Mr. Indignity" Silverman.

Bruce was my first boss. He was president of an advertising agency and I was his young and fearless new business guy. Together we travelled across the country pitching accounts. I saw how Bruce continuously got upgraded to first class, slept in rooms much larger than mine, got free meals at four star restaurants, and once (not long after 9/11) even got through airport security with nothing more than a credit card for an ID. I also saw him try to talk his way out of a speeding ticket at the Reno airport. (That didn't work so well.)

Bruce was already a legend in the world of advertising when I first met him. He had created ads and commercials for many of the world's most famous brands, including American Airlines, American Express, Hershey's, Mattel, Mercedes Benz and Shell. He served as Executive Creative Director at Ogilvy & Mather, BBDO, Bozell and Asher/Gould, and was President of the principal U.S. operation of the world's largest media planning and buying agency, Initiative. An industry leader, he was Vice Chairman of the Western region of the American Association of Advertising Agencies, and served on the AAAA national board of directors.

Effective complaint letters are like great magazine or newspaper ads. They get "the consumer" – the company the letter is addressed to – to pay attention. They make the issues clear and the benefits of responding almost impossible to ignore.

Retired from the ad business, Bruce now focuses his time on helping people write complaint letters. I already feel bad for all the company executives who are going to receive a "taught by Bruce Silverman" written complaint letter.

Their loss is your gain. Enjoy the free travel, hotel rooms, cash refunds and bananas. I certainly do.

And please, be sure to shoot us an email when you meet someone friendly and forthcoming at the Reno police department.

Kind regards,

Mario Schulzke, Publisher

How It All Began

About twenty years ago I was working at an advertising agency in Los Angeles.

My job required extensive travel, so I was – by any definition – a very frequent flyer. So frequent, in fact, that I was one of the first passengers to accumulate over 1 million miles in the American Airlines AAdvantage® frequent flyer program.

Which I enjoyed tremendously. I used the miles to fly free to Hawaii. Europe. New York. Even Australia. I gave free trips away to my kids. Sometimes I even gave miles as Christmas presents to friends.

Which meant that every mile I could acquire was tremendously valuable. So I flew American, rented from Avis, and stayed at Sheraton hotels, all to accumulate AAdvantage miles. Every one counted.

And when I found out that one of my fellow employees, "Leon A," was about to fly to New York to visit his parents, I made him an offer he couldn't refuse:

I offered to arrange for him to fly First Class. (One of the benefits of the AAdvantage program in those days was that good customers could get upgrades, even on a deeply discounted coach ticket, just by asking.) The only catch: he had to fly as *me*, and use *my* AAdvantage number. (Due to heightened security procedures, airlines today require passengers to show a photo ID at check-in. No such procedure existed in 1986.)

It was a win/win deal. Leon would get to fly First Class; I would get the 5,000 AAdvantage miles for the round trip. He didn't fly that often, and the miles were therefore much less meaningful to him than they were to me.

So off he went. A day after arriving in New York, Leon phoned me.

"I've never been in First Class! It was great! The seats are really big! And they give you hot towels! And the flight attendants are friendly! And the food is good! And I loved the champagne and orange juice! And the..."

"Calm down, my boy," I said. (I was well aware of the amenities available on American's planes to New York.) I'm glad you enjoyed the flight. Let me know when you're coming back so I can set up the First Class upgrade for you again."

"Thanks," he said. A few days later he called with his itinerary, and I dutifully arranged the upgrade.

A week passed, and Leon returned to work.

"So, how was your trip back?" I asked.

Leon's countenance darkened.

"It was awful! AWFUL. Scary. Terrible. I was almost killed!"

"What happened?" I asked. Frankly, I was expecting a joke. (Leon was a pretty funny guy. I figured the hot nuts weren't hot, or the movie was something he had already seen.)

"Well, just after we took off there was this terrible noise. A big BANG. The whole plane shuddered. Then we sort of bucked in the air like a horse!"

"God that sounds awful." (Better him than me, I couldn't help thinking.)

"The pilot came on the P.A., and even he sounded scared. He said that we were experiencing a 'mechanical problem,' and they were going to dump fuel and go back to Kennedy."

(As an experienced traveler, I damned well knew that "a mechanical problem" could be a euphemism for an engine falling off!)

"So we circled around for awhile dumping fuel, and then went back to JFK. But that was just the beginning."

"It gets worse?" I asked.

"Worse. Much worse." Leon's eyes now evoked the pained expression of a 5th century martyr being burned at the stake. "When we got off the plane there wasn't anyone there to help us!"

"Nobody?"

"Nobody! There we were… hundreds of people… our plane had nearly blown up… and nobody was there to help us get home. AND I WAS A FIRST CLASS PASSENGER!!!"

(How quickly one becomes spoiled, I thought.) Intrigued, I asked what happened next.

"Well, after about *a half hour* one – just one!!! – airline person came out and started rebooking us on other planes. I went up to the front of the line and said, 'hey, I'm a first class passenger. Do I have to wait in this stupid line? I want to get home!!!"

"And…???"

"She told me to go to the back of the line. *The back of the line!!!* I was a first class passenger and they almost killed me and then they made me go to the back of the line!"

"Awful," I said, just to commiserate.

"And when I finally got up to the stupid desk they told me that I wouldn't be able to leave for another three hours – and that I'd be in coach!!!"

I felt for him. I really did. But he needed a reality check. So I sat him down and said, "Leon. These things happen. You were never going to die. It's hard for the airline to rebook all those people… and remember, you were really on a deep discount ticket…"

"I don't give a shit!" he screamed. "I was scared and confused and I hated it and I'm never going to fly American again!"

At which point he stomped off to his office.

And I couldn't help but smile. Because at that moment, "Mr. Indignity" was born.

After all, it was *me* – not Leon – whose name was on the ticket. It was *me* – not Leon -- whose name was on the flight manifest. And it was *me* – not Leon -- whose name was on the boarding pass.

Therefore, it was *me* – not Leon – who was on the plane. And it was *me* – not Leon – who was scared and confused and hated it and might never fly American again *unless*…

Mr. Indignity Gets Indignant

I sat down that night and wrote a letter to American Airlines.

It was sort of my maiden voyage into the world of complaining. And I didn't get it right at all.

My letter was angry.

I protested. Grumbled. Moaned. Wailed. Griped. Fussed. Snarled. Whimpered.

I probably came across as some nutcase.

And then I waited for a reply.

And waited.

And waited.

After a month, I decided it was time to write a second letter.

Taking "a spoonful of sugar makes the medicine go down" lesson from Mary Poppins, I took a completely different tack. One that has worked for me over and over now for more than twenty years.

I praised with faint damn.

My letter began with a paragraph on how much *I loved and adored* American Airlines. I included the fact that I had earned over a million miles in their frequent flyer program. I also mentioned that I often recommended American to business associates, and specified American for those employees who reported to me.

Then... and only then... I started a paragraph with the words, "Which is why I was so *disappointed* when...."

I acknowledged that "mechanicals" happen (though probably less on American because of its fine maintenance operation). I saluted the flight crew for their professionalism. I underscored (again) my loyalty to the carrier.

And then I *attacked* – but ever so gently.

"….clearly, assigning *one* passenger agent to rebook an entire DC10 was inadequate and a management error. Trying to find seats on American (and other carriers) for all the passengers was a time consuming process, and frustrating for people who knew – best case – that they were going to arrive in Los Angeles very, very late. Compounding that problem was the anxiety that had been engendered by the recent adventure over Jamaica Bay. And…"

Disappointed. Chagrined. Let down. *Betrayed*.

My original, unanswered, letter had been addressed to "Director of Consumer Affairs."   My second letter was addressed very personally to Robert Crandall, Chairman of American.

One week after mailing it a letter arrived from the "office of the Chairman." In it was an apology for my discomfort… and $1,000 in the form of an American Travel Voucher.

Mr. Indignity had "cracked the code."

Postscript

When I told Leon about the Travel Voucher, he contended that since he had really been on the plane, and had been "scared shitless by the experience," and treated like "crap" by American's ground personnel at JFK," that he should get the voucher. He did have a point – but, then again, he hadn't written the letter. I had. So we split it. (Of course, when Leon used his half of the voucher, he had to fly as me… and I got the miles! Again.)

Sugar with Spice

"Praising with faint damn" is the key ingredient in Mr. Indignity's bag of tricks. "Gushing" when the response you get is all you hoped for is the second.

Here are two letters to Continental Airlines that were written in the early '90's. Note the "praise" in the first letter, and the "gush" in the second.

Mr. James V. O'Donnell
Senior Vice President, Marketing & Programming
Continental Airlines Corporation

An Appeal from a "Do the Continental" Victim

Dear Mr. O'Donnell:

I hope you can help me.

Sometime last year I opened an account at
American Savings Bank here in California. One
of my reasons for choosing ASB was their "Do
the Continental," "Buy One/Get One Free"
promotion.

As you can see, my "Get One Free" coupon,
attached, has expired. Unused.

At the time I opened the account I expected to
use the coupon for a European holiday I was
planning for the winter of 1990/91.

Unfortunately, the Gulf War intervened. Along
with thousands of other Americans, I heeded the
advice of our government and avoided
"unnecessary" travel -- especially to Europe.

(In fact, the odds of getting my "significant other" on a plane heading to Europe during the war was about as good as betting that a snowstorm would hit Houston in August.)

So -- through no fault of Continental, American Savings Bank, or myself -- I missed out on a very good deal.

In fact, I sort of feel cheated out of a vacation.

That's why I'm writing to you.

I am requesting that the validation period for the attached coupon be extended somewhat. (Three months would probably be quite fair. And I could live with restrictions, blackout dates, etc. if that would help make it happen.)

As a marketing professional, I am well aware that extending the eligibility period of a promotion that has ended is rather unusual. And I am also sensitive to the financial havoc wreaked by the war on your industry and your company.

Even so, I think there may be some good reasons for you to accommodate my request.

First, my motivation for not using the coupon in a timely manner was not perfidious. Only hindsight says that our concerns about European travel may have been overblown.

Second, you'll gain the revenue derived from the First Class (or Business Class) ticket to Europe or Australia that I'll purchase. (Every ticket counts, doesn't it?)

Third, you'll live up to the original intent of the ASB promotion... which was to generate some

trial and revenue (albeit discounted) for
yourself.

And finally, your company will win a friend. A
friend who averages 40 business flights a year;
many to Continental destinations.

I look forward to hearing from you.

Sincerely,

Bruce Silverman
Mr. Indignity

Mr. James V. O'Donnell
Senior Vice President, Marketing & Programming
Continental Airlines Corporation

Dear Mr. O'Donnell:

I wanted to personally thank you for the
<u>incredibly</u> quick response I received to my
letter to you dated June 14th.

I am quite pleased with the coupon for the free
round trip ticket sent to me by Meaghan
Affleck.

While not exactly what I expected, given the
circumstances I think it's a very fair solution
to my problem.

And as I promised, you HAVE won a friend.

I intend to fly Continental A LOT in the next
few months.

Sincerely,

19

You'll note that these letters were addressed to Mr. O'Donnell, who was at that time the marketing chief of the airline. Not an anonymous job title. The odds of a "Mr. Indignity Letter" getting its' desired result increases tremendously if the letter identifies a senior executive who can actually commit the company to something. I also went out of the way to identify the person who actually arranged my "reward." In most cases, the recipient of your letter will send a copy on to whomever it was you mentioned, which means that if you need *additional* help, you'll have someone to go to who just might remember you fondly.

Gushing should not be limited to a single letter. Once you've established a relationship, milk it!

Relationship Building

I learned the value of gushing early-on in my "Mr. Indignity" career.

I had gone on vacation to the Ritz-Carlton on Maui, and hardly anything went right. The weather was miserable (not the hotel's fault, as I pointed out in my letter); the pool was being repaired (an accident of timing); and the hotel seemed somewhat short-staffed. Compounding the bad weather, which made going to the beach all but impossible, the repairs that were taking place at the pool were very, very noisy. This (in my opinion at least) was an error of judgment by management; if the guests couldn't go to the beach, they at least should have been able to hang out by the pool in peace.

In addition, the service in the restaurant was horrible, and our room happened to be over a service entry, out of which (over a cobblestone walk) room service carts rattled early in the morning and late at night.

I carefully followed my "praise with faint damn" strategy in the opening paragraphs of the complaint letter I sent to the hotel's manager, Mr. John Toner:

Bruce Silverman
Mr. Indignity

Mr. John J. Toner
General Manager
THE RITZ-CARLTON KAPALUA

<u>"The Kapalua Blues"</u>

Dear Mr. Toner:

I'd like to share a story with you.

About three months ago I happened to be at a
cocktail reception at the Ritz-Carlton
Buckhead, in Atlanta.

Just as I was about to bite into what appeared
to be a very tasty hors d'oeuvre, it slipped
from my grasp and dropped onto my suit jacket…
leaving a very ugly stain.

I immediately went over to the bartender and
asked for a glass of club soda and a cloth
napkin. The bartender, seeing the stain,
instinctively understood that the club soda
wasn't for drinking.

"Sir," he said, "do you expect to be at the
party much longer?"

I said that I figured to be there for about an hour and a half. He nodded, and asked if I wouldn't mind going without my jacket. Considering that the meatball blob on my lapel was pretty horrific, I said that was fine with me. He took the jacket, saying that he'd get it to housekeeping to have it dry cleaned… and back to me within an hour.

I was amazed and delighted. But I wasn't a hotel guest, and told him so.

His response: "Sir, no problem. You are at *the* Ritz-Carlton. We shall take care of this."

So when we chose the Ritz-Carlton Kapalua for our vacation, our expectations were <u>very high</u>. And when it turned out to be far less than wonderful, we were especially disappointed…

The letter then went on to detail our issues with the weather, the pool, the restaurant and the clattering room service carts, and concluded with a request for some sort of compensation.

Within three days, Mr. Toner called me at my office. (A very impressive move, since my complaint letter was written on my home stationary. He had tracked me down through my travel agent!) In addition to apologizing, he invited me to spend a week at the hotel – for free!

Naturally, I took him up on his offer.

When we arrived, an assistant manager escorted us to the *Presidential Suite,* overlooking the Molokai Channel. The whales were frolicking just outside our window. Inside, I idled the early evenings away playing old Hawaiian tunes on the grand piano in the suite's living room. Every day – without fail – I was phoned by an assistant manager to make certain I was content. And although Mr. Toner's offer didn't include meals, every meal we ate at the hotel turned out to be "comped." They even picked up and returned us to the airport in the hotel's limousine!

Keep in mind the lessons of this letter:

1. **Surprise the reader.**
   Don't write it in an expectable way. Make it personable. Make it interesting. Make it intriguing…

   Keep in mind that it's likely that your letter will be read by someone – an executive assistant, most likely – before it gets read by the person you've actually addressed it to. Executive Assistants are usually very very smart people. If your letter resonates with the assistant, he or she will likely push the boss to read it!

2. **Praise first.**
   Establish that you have high expectations; that you expect the best. And prove you really have a right to your expectations. You've been a customer in the past and hope to be one in the future. You've been happy with their product or service. Be thoughtful about it…

3. **Don't linger.**
   If your letter reaches a key executive, he or she won't have all the time in the world for "a chat." Get to the point; get to the issue; get to the problem.

4. **Be reasonable.**
   Mr. Toner couldn't control the weather at Kapalua. But he could/should have recognized that if the weather was such (high winds) that the beach had to be closed, the pool simply shouldn't have been closed at the same time. (After all, what's the point of being in Hawaii at a luxury resort if you can't go to the beach *or* the pool?) That argument made sense.

5. **Be clear that you haven't written them off.**
   Mr. Toner wouldn't have had any incentive to do anything for me if my letter said "I hate you and never want to see you again!" I had concluded the letter by asking for a free night or two or some sort of discount on my next visit. That demonstrated that as disappointed as we were, we were still "fans" and wanted to return.

And, of course, never forget to follow-up a great response with a "gush!"

Bruce Silverman
Mr. Indignity

Mr. John J. Toner
General Manager
THE RITZ-CARLTON KAPALUA

Dear Mr. Toner:

In *Twelfth Night,* Shakespeare wrote: "I can no other answer make but thanks, and thanks, and ever thanks."

I wish I could be so eloquent.

Our stay at the Ritz-Carlton Kapalua last week was nothing short of <u>perfect</u>.

You have assembled a remarkable team of spirited people who add as much (if not more) to the Ritz-Carlton experience as the beauty of the property itself. Everyone: the housekeepers, pool attendants, waiters and waitresses, doormen, front desk staff, health club supervisors... *everyone*... seems to <u>want</u> to go out of their way to make you feel welcome, attended to, comfortable and happy.

Now that I'm back in Los Angeles, facing the reality of yet another deadline on an advertising campaign... smog... traffic...

sometimes snarling, unfriendly people... and a
crew of workmen trying to rebuild the part of
my house that fell down during the earthquake,
it almost seems like I was off for a week in
some sort of fantasy dreamland!

You may have saved my sanity.

You definitely saved my bank account through
your hospitality. But I intend for the Ritz-
Carlton Kapalua to recoup every dime the next
chance I get out to Maui... which I figure
will be in about three months. So I look
forward to seeing you again soon.

My thanks to you. And especially, to Shan,
who made sure all was well virtually every
day. She's a star.

Again, mahalo and aloha.

Sincerely,

"Shan" was an assistant manager, whose principal job that week
seemed to be to make sure I was content. She was a very
effective junior manager, and it seemed clear to me, bound to
move up in the Ritz-Carlton organization. So she went on my
"gush list," along with Mr. Toner.

Bruce Silverman
Mr. Indignity

Ms. Shan Kanagasingham
Assist. Dir. International Guest Services
THE RITZ-CARLTON KAPALUA

Dear Shan:

Before too many days had passed, I wanted to
thank you personally for the many courtesies
you extended to me during my visit to the
Ritz-Carlton Kapalua last week.

You <u>are</u> The Ritz-Carlton. Warm. Caring. And
always, always, professional.

By last Saturday, I was almost embarrassed
(actually, now that I think about it, I *was*
embarrassed) by all the attention I had
received from you and Mr. Toner. But as I was
leaving, I happened to see you greeting a just
arriving guest... and I realized that one of
the great things about Shan Kanagasingham is
that you seem to have the knack of treating
everyone like a VIP.

I look forward to seeing you again in a few
months when I return -- this time as a paying
guest -- to Maui and the beautiful Ritz-
Carlton.

Again, mahalo and aloha.

Sincerely,

Shan did indeed move up in the Ritz-Carlton organization. I was checking into the Ritz-Carlton Laguna Niguel later that year when she appeared with a smile. "Mr. Silverman! So nice to see you. I recognized your name on the incoming reservations list and asked the clerk to let me know the moment you arrived." It turned out that she had been promoted, and was second-in-command at the Southern California hotel. Naturally, she made certain that we were given a spectacular ocean-view room.

A year passed. And it was time for another vacation. The best way I could think of to avoid a "Mr. Indignity incident" was to go back to the Ritz!

In *addition** to making a reservation through Ritz-Carlton's reservation system, I sent Mr. Toner this note:

---

* I'm a very big believer in using the internet to make hotel reservations. More often than not, hotel websites offer the best rates, and often web-only packages that can be quite attractive. But it never hurts – in fact, it almost always *helps* – to write to your "personal contact" at a hotel to tell them you're coming and that you're looking forward to seeing them.

Bruce Silverman
Mr. Indignity

Mr. John Toner
General Manager
RITZ-CARLTON KAPALUA

Dear Mr. Toner:

The last time I wrote to you -- nearly a year ago -- I had just enjoyed a fabulous week at the Ritz-Carlton Kapalua as your guest. And, as I stated in that letter, I expected to be back "in about three months" to thank you personally for your hospitality.

Those "three months" turned into *eleven*.

Between finishing the repairs to my earthquake-messed-up house, a hectic (but ultimately, rewarding) professional year, and business trips to some of the <u>worst</u> places on the planet (try India just as the plague hit!!!), I just wasn't able to get back to Maui last year. (I <u>was</u> able to do the next best thing, though: I did get away for one long weekend at the Ritz-Carlton Laguna Niguel, where I was especially pleased to run into your former cohort, Shan Kanagasingham.)

At any rate, I wanted you to know that I <u>do</u> keep my promises. We're booked into your hotel for seven nights starting February 11th. (I'm turning 50 on February 16th, and I figured that the Ritz-Carlton Kapalua was the only place on earth where I could stomach hitting the half-century mark!)

I owe you a drink when I arrive.

Sincerely,

When we arrived at the hotel, we were immediately taken in hand by an assistant manager and escorted to a fabulous ocean-view suite. (Though not free, I was given the lowest room rate available.) On the way to the room, I commented to my wife that it was a bit chillier than I expected, and I hadn't packed a sweater.

The assistant manager must have overheard my remark.

About five minutes later, while settling into our room, there was a knock at the door. A bellhop was there with a "welcome gift" from Mr. Toner: a Ritz-Carlton sweatshirt. But that wasn't the end of the courtesies extended...

```
Bruce Silverman
Mr. Indignity
```

Mr. John Toner
General Manager
THE RITZ-CARLTON KAPALUA

Dear John:

Well, here I am again once again, writing my annual "thank you for an incredible experience last week at the Ritz-Carlton Kapalua" letter.

But what a week!!!

The old cliché, "You take the cake" *almost* applies to you. But you sent <u>me</u> the cake (!!!) (Not to mention the lovely bottle of champagne) on my birthday. So I guess I can't use it to express my appreciation to you for making our visit to Maui so extra special.

Webster's New World Dictionary defines the word "Ritz" as "luxurious, fashionable, and elegant." I suspect that someday, when a dictionary editor gets around to defining "Ritz-Carlton Kapalua," they'll start with "luxurious, etc.," but they'll <u>add</u> "extraordinarily friendly and hospitable" to properly define what you're all about.

34

Your people are simply the best.

And as for you... well, despite the paragraph above, you DO take the cake!

Nancy and I can't wait to get back to Maui. See you soon.

Aloha,

By now, I was on a first-name basis with John Toner. The fabled Shan had departed for other Ritz-Carltons. But she was ably replaced by a young woman named Karen Clancy... someone clearly worth cultivating...

Bruce Silverman
Mr. Indignity

Ms. Karen Clancy
Guest Recognition Coordinator
THE RITZ-CARLTON KAPALUA

Dear Karen:

There is a certain culture shock that one has
to deal with <u>after</u> a week under your extra-
special care at the Ritz-Carlton Kapalua.

- Upon arrival at LAX there is nobody with a
  smiling face to greet you, hang a lei
  around your neck, and lead you off to a
  fabulous ocean-front suite.

- If it's chilly, no one brings you a
  sweatshirt.
- You don't get calls asking if everything is
  <u>perfect</u>.

And birthday cakes and bottles of champagne do
not magically appear in your living room.

Culture shock.... and it's all your fault!

Nancy and I will either have to adapt to life
back here in LaLaLand... or return to Maui and
the Ritz-Carlton as soon as possible.

(I think we'll opt for the latter.)

Thanks so much for your incredible
hospitality. You made a special week extra
special for us.

Aloha,

P.S. Be on the lookout for a package sent
under separate cover) for you.

Karen had mentioned to me that *Seinfeld* was her favorite
television show. I happened to live near the studio where *Seinfeld*
was shot. So I visited the studio gift shop, bought a *Seinfeld*
baseball cap, and sent it to her as a token of my appreciation. I
figured that for the cost of a cap, I'd probably end up with another
ocean-view suite for the price of a regular room on our next visit.
And I was right!

Of course, the Ritz-Carlton "won," too. They turned an unhappy
customer into a very happy – and even more importantly, into a
very <u>regular</u> customer.

Smart businesses "get it." They understand the concept of
relationship building. That's why nearly every airline, hotel chain
and car rental company operates a "Frequent User" club.

In a commoditized world, these "Loyalty Programs" provide a way for customers to think of themselves as "members of marketer's family." And, as happens in every family, sometimes a family member needs to be "hugged."

An appropriate response to a well crafted complaint letter is "the hug." A free room… a travel voucher… they're "hugs!" And hugs aren't easily forgotten.

Unrequited Anger

There are times when unrequited anger is the only effective strategy. This particularly applies in dealing with oddball merchants. Being gentle and civilized *doesn't* apply to them. Get what you want and get going. No gushing either. It's meaningless to them and therefore useless to you.

The letter that follows was written to the head of a company that was selling (way back when) VERY high-tech gadgets. It's very long... and a lot of it deals very specifically with technical problems. Even I don't think you should read the whole thing! But there's an important lesson in its style:

Don't be afraid to be specific... to go "punch for punch"... to prove that you've got a real beef, that the problem is theirs (not yours) and that you've done your best to get something to work.

A long letter is proof positive that a) you know what you're talking about. And, b) you're truly angry and frustrated.

(I have to admit that as I read the letter today, many years after I wrote it, I'm amazed at how excited I was about the "advanced and mysterious" computer accessories that I had purchased...)

Bruce Silverman
Mr. Indignity

Mr. Drew Alan Kaplan
President
DAK Industries Incorporated

"Promises Not Kept"

Dear Mr. Kaplan:

This is a complaint.

I believe I have been the victim of some very
misleading advertising. And since the
advertising in question was published under
your "byline," I have decided to write to you
personally, rather than to some "Customer
Service Representative," or Advertising
Manager.

Some months ago, very impressed with the
promises made in your catalog regarding the
Fax\Modem device, I drove out to your retail
store on a Saturday, and bought the product.

The young man on the floor was quite
enthusiastic about the ability of the
Fax\Modem to do all that was said about it in
your ad.

So I installed it.

> You can fax any document you write with any word processing program. Plus, you can fax Epson FX-compatible graphics. And, if you have a page or hand scanner, you can fax logos, signatures, invoices or any document not inside your PC.

Figure 1 -- *Your description of the ability of the DAK Fax\Modem to transmit any document. Perhaps a slight overstatement?*

I expected to be able to Fax out any of my WordPerfect Files just as they "appeared" in my computer. To me, a Fax means *facsimile*. Therefore, I expected italics to appear as *italics*...bold face to appear as **bold face**...LARGE TYPE to appear as LARGE TYPE.

I expected that any graphic images that might be incorporated in my document to appear as a graphic image in my fax. In fact, based on your ad, I expected the Fax\Modem to be a 90's version of Mr. Eastman's incredible Kodak camera... "Push a button, we do the rest."

Which leads me to **COMPLAINT NUMBER 1**. The DAK Fax\Modem is a long way from a Kodak.

The Fax\Modem transmits *Text Files*. But it ignores printer commands. So instead of sending a *FACSIMILE* of the document I prepared, it transmits the text only. In a standard typeface. Unadorned. No italics.

No bold face. No large type.

As for sending graphics... well, *maybe* it can. But it sure can't send "Epson FX-compatible graphics" simply and easily. If you've read the instructions on how to capture a graphic and transmit a graphic via the BFAX routine, then you know that very few people will ever bother to try that very complex procedure. I tried it once. When I tried to incorporate a graphic, which I expected to be part of a single page document, the fax ended up as two pages, with the graphic as the second page, following the text on page one.

Now let's get to **COMPLAINT NUMBER 2.**

Your ad hailed the "Background" feature of the Fax\Modem, which would enable me to work normally at the computer and send or receive faces at the same time.

That sounded great!

Unfortunately, while you might be able to let it run in the background with *some* programs, it won't run correctly with most. When I tried the background

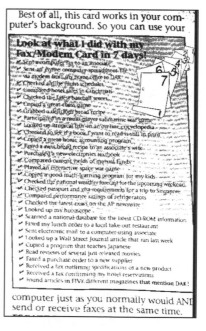

program as I used WordPerfect 5.1, an attempted Fax transmission resulted in an "unanswered" phone followed by my computer

seizing up. In the inimitable words of the
DAK Software Support person, "WordPerfect is a
Ram Hog. You can't run Fax in the background
with it."

Well, I, along with hundreds of thousands of
other computer users, use WordPerfect 5.1. So
despite your promise, I can't write and
monitor for Faxes at the same time. Now
that's not exactly a life-threatening
problem... but once again, the product didn't
live up to its advertising, either.

On to **COMPLAINT NUMBER 3**. Once I determined
that I wasn't going to be able to transmit
real *facsimiles*, I decided to take your advice
(via ad), and get a hand scanner, so I could
sort of send "pseudo" facsimiles.

I bought a Mars 105 Hand Scanner from you.
According to the manual I could combine
graphic and text files into a single page
document. So I scanned my letterhead,
creating a pcx file; then scanned my
signature, creating a second pcx file; and
finally attempted to combine them along with
text files from a short WordPerfect 5.1
document, into one, single page Fax.

But it turned out to be a THREE page document.
Page One; the letterhead. Page two; the text.
Page three (you got it); the signature.

So I called your Software support line again.
(I won't even go into how hard they are to
reach. Suffice to say, it ain't exactly like
calling a major software company.)

per-inch) scanner, you can 'lift' almost any
graphic piece of art, photo or text, modify
it to your exact specifications and incorporate it into anything you write.

It seems
that the
problem is
that

Scankit, the software that runs the Scanner, can't *size* a graphic. It stores everything as a full page.

So if I simply scan a little note, and then attempt to Fax it, it will get sent as a full page --- hugely enlarged.

I then asked the obvious question: "How do I re-size a scanned image?" And I'll bet that the answer would surprise even **you**!

You can't!

It seems that the sizing feature in PC Paintbrush doesn't work. ("It worked in the prototype, I guess. I suppose we just didn't test the actual production copies we received," said the DAK Software Support person.)

The Software Support person went on to say that you *used to* ship a software package with the Scanner called HALO, which EASILY sized scanned images. He offered to send the Halo software to me. No charge!

Great.

Except it arrived without instructions. And when I called again (BUSY SIGNAL, BUSY SIGNAL, BUSY SIGNAL...) I discovered that you no longer have manuals for Halo. So although I have the disks, I can't figure out how to load the program or execute it.

Which, of course, causes me to make **COMPLAINT NUMBER 4** to you:

Not to be denied, I decided to believe the copy in your "Rip-Off Artist" ad and attempt to integrate the scanned images I've made with

my Mars 105 Scanner with my word processing
documents.

(Just in case you've forgotten what you said, I've

> So, whether the image you're heisting is black and white, or in color, you'll always capture a great-looking black and white copy.
> Once you've scanned an image, you can incorporate it into any good word processing, paint program and desktop publishing program like WordStar®, Microsoft Word®, GEM Desktop Publishing®, WordPerfect (5.0)®, MultiMate Advantage II®, PageMaker®, and Windows Paint®. It's a breeze.

scanned it into this

document. It appears just to the left.)

As you've seen, the Scankit PCX software seems
to do a pretty good job with high contrast
text.

On the other hand, it sort of doesn't live up
to its advertising promise:

> The Rip-Off Artist bounces a newly-improved yellow-green (not red) LCD light off the page you're scanning and precisely measures how much light comes back (a yellow-green scan beam produces superb black & white images from color photographs).

In fact, if you tried to scan in a "picture of
the company president and instantly place it
on brochures, business correspondence or hand
books," the person doing the scanning would
likely piss the company president off pretty
good.

Here are some samples of scanned images
imported into my WordPerfect 5.1 program.

They were printed with an Epson dot matrix printer.

This was scanned right from your brochure. It appears here only slightly smaller than the original.

The original is a pretty good 4x6 color photo.

Think "superb" is a bit of an over statement?

So to sum it all up...

1. Your copy for the Fax\Modem overstates its capabilities. It receives well; sends in a rudimentary way.

2. The background program is barely useful.

3. Despite what the Fax/Modem manual says, you can't combine PCX and text files on one page. And graphics files can't be sized.

4. The quality of output from the scanner, particularly as it applies to color photos, is quite low. (Have you any idea why the

photo on the right above turned out like it
did? Why did that odd pattern develop?)
5. When imported into WordPerfect 5.1, the
quality of the scanned images deteriorates
even more.

Mr. Kaplan, you are a *great* copywriter. (I've
been writing advertising for some of the
biggest clients at the largest advertising
agencies in the world for nearly 25 years and
I can't hold a candle to you.) But you ought
to make a better effort to get the facts
straight about your products.

You're probably wondering why I simply haven't
packed everything up and returned stuff to
you. The answer: simple research. Nobody's
FAX\Modem does what you implied yours would
do. So what I've got is about as good as is
on the market.

As for the scanner... well, to tell the truth,
I HATE opening up my computer. I'd have to
open it up to pull the card out if I was going
to return it to you. And besides, I'm not
sure that any hand scanner will do what you
led me to believe yours could do. So to hell
with it. I'll just write it off as a bad
mail-order experience. Maybe you'll at least
apologize. Or dredge up the instructions for
Halo (although I doubt it does what your guy
claimed. Nothing else you sell seems to do
quite what you claim...)

Sincerely,

Think my letter was too long?   Think again.   When your complaint is that detailed, the reader knows you're *serious*.   Especially if your arguments are unarguable.

Besides that little piece of letter-writing logic, there was another reason for the length of the letter. DAK used long, long copy in his ads. In essence, my complaint letter fought fire with fire.

Without comment – not even a note – I received a check for the value of everything I had bought from DAK!

Ironically, DAK went bankrupt shortly thereafter. No great surprise – but at least, I collected before the firm's demise.

DAK was a tiny operation.   Fry's Electronics takes an entirely different tack: they operate "big box" stores; retailing giants that measure floor space by the acre.

Bruce Silverman
Mr. Indignity

Mr. Randy Fry
Fry's, Inc.

"The Opposite of "Empowerment"

Dear Mr. Fry:

I am writing to you because I recently experienced one of the <u>worst</u> retail experiences of my life. And it happened at your store in Burbank on Sunday, September 8th.

On August 18th I purchased a new Compaq computer (plus accessories) at Fry's.

To "sweeten the deal," and match a similar Compaq being sold at CompUSA, the manager of the computer department agreed to reduce the cost of the computer by the amount needed to pay for an additional 1MB of video RAM. I therefore bought the computer (and the RAM chips) at Fry's, instead of CompUSA.

However, when I got home and opened the computer, I discovered that I had been given the wrong RAM chips.

So the following Saturday (August 25th), I went back to the store to exchange the chips. I was treated very courteously; the "Person in Charge" was helpful. He determined which chips I really needed, and instructed the sales associate in the Components Department to special order the chips from Compaq. I was told that the chips would probably be available in three or four days and that I would receive a call when they arrived.

He wrote the following note on a copy of my original quote:

> "*(Our mistake). Customer was given the wrong Video RAM chip. The one he needs is a special order item. Freddie Ascencio will special order item and when item comes in, we will adjust it down to $24.95. The customer cost will be -0-. Gary (I can't quite make out his last name) #23647.*"

A full week passed without a call.

So on Sunday, September 1st, I called the store and asked to speak to the Components Department. *I got hung up on four times* before I got through.

I asked if the chips had come in.

I got the distinct impression that the sales associate hadn't the faintest idea what I was talking about. (This despite having a "PLU number" for the special order.)

The sales associate promised to have Freddie Ascencio, who I gather is in charge of that department, call the buying office on Tuesday to check on the order. I was told that Freddie

would call me on Tuesday to provide an update.
(Monday was Labor Day.)

Tuesday came and went. No call. So did
Wednesday. And Thursday. No calls.

Finally, I tried calling on Friday. Again, I
experienced a series of hang-ups when I asked
to be transferred to the Components Department.
After *six* tries, I gave up.

So on Sunday, September 8th, I called the store
and asked to speak to the Manager. I told my
story to whomever it was that answered the
phone. I was <u>promised</u> that the Manager would
call me back within an hour.

An hour came and went. A *second* hour came and
went.

I called again. *Someone else* answered the
phone. I told my whole story all over again.
I was told that a Manager would call back
shortly.

And lo and behold, someone did call. And I was
told that the chips were in. (Why nobody
bothered to call me when they arrived remains a
mystery.)

So I drove over to the store, expecting the
exchange process to take fifteen or twenty
minutes.

It took **TWO HOURS.**

First I had to return the original chips.
That, as I'm sure you know, involves seeing a
clerk near the front door, who has to get
approvals from two or three different people
before completing the transaction.

Then I had to go to the counter to get the correct chips.

I showed the clerk my credit slip and the note that Gary, the "Person in Charge" had written the first time I had returned to the store to try to exchange the chips.

Your clerk said, "He's not here. I can't accept this."

I was incredulous. I said, "Whether he's here or not you will too accept it! He didn't write this as an individual; he wrote it as an official of Fry's!"

This bit of logic seemed to overwhelm the clerk.

So off she went with the note to see a supervisor.

Fifteen minutes passed.

She came back to the counter to tell me that it would take at least 30 minutes (!!!) for her to get an approval.

So I told her that I would wander around the store while she waited for approval.

(I actually ended up finding a few items that I needed. So although my time was being wasted, you guys actually ended up making a few more bucks on me.)

Twenty-five minutes passed. I went back to the counter. The clerk had just returned, too. "Okay," she said. "Now I have to get the chips." She headed towards the cage. Another twenty minutes (and I'm exaggerating) went by before she returned with them.

All in all, an hour and forty-five minutes had passed. An hour and forty-five minutes to deal with the fact that Fry's had screwed up in the first place by carelessly giving me the wrong components.

But the story doesn't end there.

Remember those "miscellaneous items" that I picked up while killing time? I had to pay for them.

So I headed towards checkout. Frankly, I was fuming.

The clerk rang up my purchases. Then the computers went down. Five or six minutes passed.

I couldn't stand it any more. I asked the clerk if he could provide me with the name and address of the "Chief Executive Officer of Fry's."

The clerk said he had to go ask his supervisor to get that information. That took another five minutes.

When the clerk returned to the counter, he said that he couldn't give me the information I had requested. That he "wasn't allowed."

I asked to see the supervisor.

The supervisor -- rather begrudgingly, if body language means anything -- sauntered over.

"I'd like the name and mailing address of the Chief Executive Officer of Fry's," I asked.

"We can't give that out," he replied.

"I don't believe you," I said.

"Well, why do you want it?" he responded.

"That is my business," I said. "But if you must know, I want to complain about the service at this store."

"Well, they don't like us to give that information out," said the supervisor.

"That is idiotic," I said. I pointed out that Fry's corporate office address was probably pretty easily accessible through one of the Internet telephone directories.

The supervisor, Lance Marquis, acknowledged that I was probably right, and provided the address for this letter.

(I ended up having to look up the zip code myself. He didn't know it.)

So, to sum this sorry episode up, I had to visit your store on three separate occasions, make more than 10 phone calls, and have two hours of my weekend ruined to actually get my new computer system to operate the way it was supposed to when I bought it from Fry's.

I've enjoyed shopping at Fry's. In the past year I've personally bought about $10,000 worth of computer equipment and accessories from your stores in Woodland Hills, Manhattan Beach and Burbank. More importantly, my company has

probably spent another $10,000-$15,000 with
you.

No more.

The most precious thing a retailer provides a
customer is NOT the merchandise, or the lowest
price. It's the *service experience.*

That's what brings customers back.

And in my case, the Fry's service experience
has made me a very loyal CompUSA customer.

Sincerely,

P.S. I know this letter is pretty long. But I
figured I ought to waste at least a *little bit*
of your time, since you wasted a *lot* of mine.

Fry's sent me a gift certificate for $250.00. I forgave them.

(And their service does seem to have improved.)

Chutzpah

Professional Complainers Toolkit

"Chutzpah" is a Yiddish word that is used to describe outrageous acts. The best example I've ever heard of for "Chutzpah" was the case of the boy who killed his parents, who then threw himself on the mercy of the court because he was an orphan.

This incident – in which I had absolutely no right to complain at all – is the height of chutzpah. But it resulted in American Airlines sending me TWO free First Class tickets to Europe!

Bruce Silverman
Mr. Indignity

Mr. Robert Crandall
Chairman
American Airlines

How I Got Tricked Into a Long Freeway Drive

Dear Mr. Crandall:

I have a complaint about a very unhappy
experience I had on a British Airways flight
this past weekend that was a result of bad
advice by an American Airlines Reservations
Agent.

I called the American Gold AAdvantage desk in
early July to book a free AAdvantage trip on BA
(for September). I had no trouble booking my
L.A.-London segment, but I was told that BA was
sold-out of first-class seats on both their
London-LAX flights for the day I wanted to
return.

The Reservation Agent than told me that there
were two seats available on BA's London-San
Diego trip. She then went on to explain that
the San Diego flight and the L.A. flight were

one and the same; that the aircraft would stop
first in L.A., and then go on to San Diego.
(Apparently, BA was blocking seats for San
Diego passengers, which explained why they were
"sold out" to L.A. but not to San Diego.)

Your agent further explained to me that all of
the passengers, and their baggage, would be
required to get off the airplane in L.A. to
clear U.S. immigration and customs. She then
suggested that we go through immigration and
customs in L.A., and simply go home.

Which sounded like a pretty good idea.

So there we were, happily ensconced in seats 1A
and 1B last Sunday, flying somewhere over the
western United States, almost home, when the BA
purser made the following announcement: "San
Diego passengers will be required to stay on
the airplane while the aircraft is on the
ground in L.A."

I *nearly jumped* out of my seat.

I ran back to ask what she meant. She
explained: "San Diego passengers aren't
permitted to leave the aircraft."

"But don't we have to clear customs in Los
Angeles?" I asked, hoping she was confused.

"Oh, no. You clear customs in *San Diego*. It's
much faster than having to unload your luggage
in LAX and then having to reload it for the
short flight to San Diego!"

She was soooooo pleased about sharing news
about this procedure that I can only describe
the look on her face as bucolic!

Oh joy.

So much for your Reservation Agent's idea.

Frankly, had I known in advance that we were
actually going to be required to go on to San
Diego, I wouldn't be writing to you. I would
have made arrangements, in advance, to get home
comfortably.

But because I relied on your agent's
suggestion, the limo that I had arranged to
meet us in L.A. had nobody to pick up (though I
still got a $125 bill!!!), and I found myself
paying for a Hertz car ($79) and subjecting
myself to a three hour drive up a crowded
freeway after a thirteen hour trip!

Somebody needs to tell the reservation agents
to get their facts straight before they make
"helpful" suggestions that *don't work*.

And frankly, somebody ought to apologize to me
for my inconvenience.

Sincerely,

American's response was to send me vouchers good for two first class tickets to any of their European destinations. So not only did I fly first class for free to Europe once – I ended up flying twice.

It was an amazing reaction; one even I can't figure out. I would have been happy with some sort of acknowledgement. In fact, I would have been totally satisfied if they had sent me a voucher just to cover the cost of the car rental and limousine. Two First Class ticket vouchers were beyond belief! So the moral of the story is, "Chutzpah is good." Use it.

Ask for the Order

As every salesperson knows, you must never be shy about asking for the order. This bit of advice also applies to Mr. Indignity letters.

I wrote the following letter for my wife, who — just to preserve her sanity — we'll refer to as "Mrs. Indignity."

Mr. John Indrieri, General Manager
THE REGENT BEVERLY WILSHIRE HOTEL

A Disconcerting Error

Dear Mr. Indrieri:

I am writing to you because a number of my
friends and business associates, with whom I
shared the story detailed below, seemed
astonished that the sort of thing that I'm
about to relate to you could have happened at
a quality hotel like the Regent Beverly
Wilshire Hotel.

Just about a month ago I met my friend, the
author "P.Q.," for a quick lunch at your
coffee shop/cafe. (I frequently take my
clients -- I'm a sales executive with a radio
station -- to your hotel for breakfast or
lunch. Ms. Q, whose latest book is scheduled
for publication this month by Simon &
Schuster, is also a frequent guest in your
restaurants. In fact, she often schedules
press interviews at your hotel.)

Lunch was fine. What came next wasn't.

When the bill was presented, Ms. Q put her
credit card down. I followed with cash. Our
intent was to split the check; to pay 50% with
her credit card, 50% with my cash. The waiter
took the credit card *and* the cash, moments
later returning with the credit card voucher
and change for my cash. Ms. Q signed the
voucher, adding an appropriate tip; I left my
share of the tip in cash.

About a week later, Ms. Q and I were having
dinner with friends when she asked me if I had
paid for my lunch that day at the Regent
Beverly Wilshire. Somewhat taken aback, I
said, "Of course I did. I left cash." Ms. Q
said, "that's what I thought. But they
charged my credit card for <u>100 percent</u> of the
lunch... and the tip I wrote in was for 20% of
the total indicated on the voucher. Which
means that the waiter undoubtedly *pocketed*
your cash!"

At first we both felt pretty foolish. Ms. Q
said, "I guess I should pay closer attention
to the total before I sign a credit card
voucher." I actually thought the incident
bordered on comical: the waiter had gotten a
helluva tip!

But as I mentioned earlier, my friends and
business associates, when told this story,
were appalled. They felt you should know
about it.

The issue, of course, is whether or not the
concept of "caveat emptor" -- *let the buyer
beware* -- need apply at a property like the
Regent Beverly Wilshire.

I wish I could believe that this incident was a simple mistake by an overworked waiter. But frankly, neither Ms. Q nor I think it was a mistake. We think the waiter realized that we had been a bit careless in not reviewing the credit card voucher and decided to take advantage of us.

I don't know what you can do to compensate us for this incident. But if nothing else, you might want to find a way to ensure that other guests aren't victimized by these kinds of "mistakes" in the future.

Sincerely,

Mrs. Indignity

The highlighted sentence above may appear rather subtle to some. But it was clearly recognized by the hotel management as "asking for the order." They invited Mrs. I, her friend Ms. Q, Q's significant other, and me to a complimentary dinner in their luxury dining room.

At the risk of overkill (and by now, you've probably figured out that I don't believe there is such a thing as overkill), it is appropriate at this point to reiterate some of the key ingredients in successful complaint letter writing:

1.
Always write to a person, not to an institution. It's easy to find out the appropriate name. Do it and use it.

2.
Praise with faint damn. As in the letter above, "...a number of my friends and business associates...seemed astonished that the sort of thing that I'm about to relate to you could have happened at a

quality hotel like the Regent Beverly Wilshire Hotel." Gush when appropriate.

3.
Build a relationship.

4.
Only be angry if the nature of the malefactor is such that you're sure that the only thing they'll ever respond to is "yelling."

5.
Do not be afraid to write long letters. They'll know you're serious.

6.
Ask for the order.

Check the out the letter that follows. It scores on every point.

Bruce Silverman
Mr. Indignity

Mr. Thomas Bradshaw
President
Windstar Sail Cruises

<u>Taking the Wind out of *our* Sails</u>

Dear Mr. Bradshaw:

Last week, we returned to California after
completing a Venice/Rome cruise on the WIND
STAR.

In many ways, it was an extraordinary
experience.

The Wind Star (ship) is, in a word, beautiful.
And the Windstar "concept" is equally lovely.

That's why we thought we should write to you.
Because our experience aboard the ship just
didn't live up to the "concept." <u>But it could
have</u>.

As we're sure you know, in just about all
aspects of life, the difference between good
and great usually lies in the *details*.

Here are the details that went wrong on our cruise.

1. <u>Many of the crewmembers were unhappy, unmotivated, and, in a couple of cases, downright surly</u>.

We were told that your company was replacing most of the crew with either Filipinos or Indonesians (the story varied from crewmember to crewmember).

The crew on our cruise was, therefore, about to be fired. And they were vocal about their unhappiness. In a couple of cases, they shared their unhappiness by being unfriendly, unresponsive, or worse.

A luxury environment calls for a high degree of service. The crew, due to their negative attitudes, often made us feel <u>unwelcome</u>. That was not exactly what we had bargained for.

Incidentally, two crewmembers overtly solicited tips for themselves.

2. <u>The ship seemed to be short supplied</u>.

There were fewer than 50 deckchairs for over 100 passengers. And there wasn't a chair pad for every chair. (The chairs are rather uncomfortable without the pads). There was no crewmember assigned to help supervise the stern deck. Result: passengers "rushed" to "reserve" deckchairs early in the morning; passengers who showed up on deck after 10 a.m. couldn't find seating! The gift-shop inventory was very thin. We were told that "it was the end of the season." Maybe so. But it wasn't the end of *our* season!

3. <u>We felt nickel and dimed</u>.

Our understanding of the terms of the cruise was that other than for laundry and alcoholic beverages, there were no "extras." Yet we were charged for <u>basic</u> shore transportation; for example, to get from the dock to Taormina town, or into Corfu town, we faced $20 per ticket "extras." Frankly, we'd suggest building those charges into the basic rate for passage. We'd rather not know that a ten-minute bus ride to see what it was we came to see was costing us <u>extra</u>. It's incredibly irritating. Incidentally, we also think that charging for soft drinks (as opposed to alcoholic beverages) is also "chintzy." Even airline *coach* passengers don't have to pay for a Coca-Cola!

4. <u>Paying for shore transfers in advance was foolish</u>.

We paid $64 each to Windstar for transportation from Civitavecchia to Rome Airport at the time we booked our cruise. The same transportation was offered to passengers who hadn't booked in advance for $40!

<u>Some additional thoughts</u>: it might be a good idea for Windstar to provide passengers embarking in Venice with information about how to get to the pier, and what to do once they get there. For example, when we arrived, there was no Windstar representative at the Water Taxi landing. Not knowing any better, we struggled with our bags and carried them all the way down to the ship (quite a haul) --

where we were told they had to be "checked" back at the landing! The confusion was not in keeping with the gracious luxury experience we anticipated.

Lastly, shipboard communication was rather sloppy. On the morning we were scheduled to arrive at Capri (generally regarded as a highlight of the trip by the passengers), we sailed on past the island for about three-quarters of an hour before someone thought to make an announcement that due to weather problems we were going to have to moor off Sorrento and transfer to Capri via Hydrofoil. Ultimately, the day was well handled... the announcement delay just seemed...*sloppy*. *It was as if the passengers didn't count for much.*

I wish we could say that our experience on The Wind Star was all that we hoped it would be. Perhaps our expectations were <u>too high</u>. But we don't think so. It appears that the delivery was just <u>too low</u>.

Incidentally, on our last night aboard, service completely collapsed in the dining room. It was difficult to order a bottle of wine... and impossible to get the wine poured after the first glass. A second bottle? No chance. The waiter clearly couldn't have cared less. And even Eric, the dining room manager (who is quite wonderful, by the way) couldn't seem to wake the waiter from his torpor.

How sad that our "trip of a lifetime" ended on such a negative note.

I think it would be appropriate for Windstar to consider compensating us for this less than sensational experience. Don't you agree?

Sincerely,

"Appalled," (their word, not mine), Windstar came across with two free tickets for their South Pacific (Tahiti, Moorea, Bora Bora) cruise. We were upgraded to the "Owner's Cabin" when we boarded. A bottle of *Cristal* champagne was on ice, with a very nice "welcome aboard" note from Mr. Bradshaw.

Living in a Sitcom

The letter that follows is one of my favorites. I almost didn't write it because the situation I experienced was so absurd that it bordered on comedic... and I wasn't sure if anyone – especially the President of an airline – would believe it. In fact, it reads like a Sitcom script... you can almost see this happening to Jerry Seinfeld, or Kramer. But it didn't; it happened to *me*.

JetBlue Airways has gotten its share of bad press because of a series of flights that had to be delayed on the ground with the passengers stuck on the airplane without anything to eat or drink for many hours.

This isn't about that.

Bruce Silverman
Mr. Indignity

Mr. David Neeleman
Founder and CEO
JetBlue Airways

A **HEAVY** Disappointment Report

Dear Mr. Neeleman:

I suspect that I'm like a lot of your
customers: I had heard all sorts of good
things about JetBlue, and had it in my head to
"give it a try one of these days."

My opportunity finally came last week when I
found myself needing to make a quick trip to
New York. I checked fares on AA, DL and UA,
didn't like what I saw, then checked your
fares and schedule from Long Beach, *liked* what
I saw, and booked the trip. (16 Oct; Flight
22; Long Beach/JFK.)

And when I got on the plane, I thought I'd
<u>really</u> like it. Big bins. Nice leather
seats. Televisions. I was even in an exit
row, with extra leg room…

Then my seatmate arrived.

He was easily 400 pounds.

In fact, he was *so* big that he couldn't fit
into his aisle seat at all unless the arm rest
stayed up. Which meant that in addition to
his own seat, he took up a significant portion
of *my* middle seat... with me in it! He took up
so much space that I couldn't use my tray
table. Believe it or not, to change TV
channels, I had to ask the people in the row
behind me to push the buttons on the upright
arm rest!

It was sort of like a scene from an old Marx
Brothers movie: the very very huge man in the
aisle seat... me, squished in the middle... the
guy by the window who knew there was no way he
was going to be able to go to the bathroom
until we got to JFK... the nice lady in row 13
serving as human TV remote control.

But it wasn't funny; it was painful. The big
guy was just too big for one seat.

I felt cheated. I paid for a seat, but only
got to sit in half of it. For more than five
hours.

I know that it's very difficult to accommodate
situations like this one, particularly on a
full flight. I think that at least a few
airlines are either denying seating to "extra
large" people if they can't find an empty seat
for them to sit next to, or making them buy
two seats; I don't know if JetBlue has a
policy on this issue.

But as an airline that clearly wants to
differentiate itself by providing a
perceptively better comfort experience, you
need a policy. It's fundamentally unfair to

squish your passengers.   (That's Southwest's
job!)

I do believe that some sort of compensation
for my pain would be appropriate.

Sincerely,

JetBlue has one of the best customer complaint response
mechanisms I've ever seen. (They are either extremely customer
centric – or they receive so many complaints that they've got the
response thing down to a science.)

Either way, I truly admire their reaction to my letter. I received an e-
mail from JetBlue just three days after I mailed my letter to them. It
was definitely personalized; it addressed my specific complaint (by
saying they don't throw overly large people off their airplanes), but
they demonstrated empathy by providing me with a code for a free
flight.   (They pointed out that it appeared that I didn't have a
complaint about the return leg of my New York trip. so the free ticket
was only one way, but still very fair.)

Lessons from this letter:

1. It starts with praise.

2. It clearly states the problem in a way that's hard not to
   empathize with.

3. It asks for compensation.

4. It worked.

How to complain when you're so angry you never intend to deal with those bastards again

Every once in awhile something happens that is so awful that you say to yourself, "I hate them and I'll never deal with them again."

If so, go for broke.

Fire and brimstone were probably beaming out of my eyes when I wrote the letter that follows. I was so angry that I broke two of my own rules: I made no effort to find out the name of the person I was writing to... and I didn't ask for anything!

Bruce Silverman
Mr. Indignity

DELTA AIR LINES, INC.
Consumer Affairs

To whom it may concern:

I am writing this complaint letter to you
while sitting in the <u>American</u> Airlines
Admirals Club at Hartsfield Airport.

I arrived here about an hour ago on your
flight 1034 from Tallahassee. I was *supposed*
to connect to your 3:30 p.m. flight to Los
Angeles. The flight was canceled due to a
mechanical problem.

These things happen.

However, what happened next <u>shouldn't</u> have
happened.

After learning that I was going to arrive in
Los Angeles two hours late -- and further
learning that although I was a full-fare first
class passenger that there were no first class
seats on flight 189 available -- I asked one
of your passenger service representatives if I

could kill the waiting time in your Crown
Room. His answer was "no."

I pressed the issue a bit. After all, I had
paid $1,963 for my ticket. I was going to be
late. And I was going to have to fly coach,
despite paying for a first class ticket. An
hour or so in the club seemed a reasonable
accommodation for a "distressed passenger."

"No."

He explained that he would be forced to take
three days off without pay if he "slipped me
in."

I told him that it seemed pretty dumb to me to
send an already inconvenienced passenger over
to the warm confines of your leading
competitor. He said -- and I quote -- "Are
you prepared to pay me for the three days
off?"

Since I wasn't, I strolled on down to the
American club (which I've belonged to for many
years) and started writing this letter.

Now I have to admit that I've felt a bit let
down by Delta lately.

Last week, on another full-fare first class
round-trip, your flight DL007 (January 27)
from Tampa to LAX was more than two hours late
getting away from the gate. On January 19th,
while flying (you guessed it: full-fare first-
class) from Orlando to LAX on DL171, I arrived
about an hour and thirty minutes late. Now
that I think about it, I can't remember a
single Delta round-trip I've taken lately that
didn't have operational problems!

So here I am at the (American Airlines)
Admiral's Club.

I'm supposed to fly to Europe next week on
Delta. (Full fare, first class. BIG money!
With three of my business associates... all of
who report to me.) What would you do if you
were me?

Hey! I'll be darned. American goes to
Europe! (Did you know that?)

Sincerely,

cc: M. Behringer-Harris, QST Travel Group

"cc:" stands for "carbon copy (a bit of an anachronism these days;
when was the last time you even saw carbon paper???). But it's
still used to note that you're copying someone – and in this case, it
was a great weapon.

M. Behringer-Harris happens to be the branch manager of the
large travel agency with whom my company did business. And
airlines have a love/hate relationship with travel agencies. They
hate having to pay commissions to them... but they also know that
they steer business their way.

I never got a direct response from Delta from this letter. But I did hear from the travel agency, who called me when they read it to ask for more details, and I heard back from them with *their* resolution to the problem: a travel voucher worth $750. Which just happened to be the cost of joining the Delta Crown Room Club.

I had no interest in joining the Crown Room (or flying Delta again if I could help it), so I gave the voucher to my daughter, who used it to visit her mother in Florida.

Small Stuff

No good complainer should ignore small issues. There is nothing too small to complain about. Nothing!

This letter, addressed to a local coffee shop, complained about *coffee cup take-out* lids. I wrote it for my wife.

Mr. Mäni Nial
Mr. Larry Maiman
Mäni's Bakery

<u>Stained in the City</u>

Gentlemen:

I'm writing to you to let you know that Mäni's
Bakery is a favorite of mine. I frequently
stop on my way to work to pick up coffee and a
muffin or special treats for my co-workers.

But unfortunately, this is <u>not</u> a note of
praise. Rather, it is one of painful
disappointment.

About two weeks ago I experienced an
unpleasant incident at Mäni's, which, at the
time, I considered a simple oversight on your
part.

When I ordered my usual coffee "to go," I
noticed that you had replaced your "tried and
true" plastic coffee lids with lids of a new
design. Unfortunately, the new lid didn't fit
your coffee cup very well. It <u>leaked</u>. Badly.

In fact, no matter how hard I tried to adjust it, the lid continued to leak.

Within minutes of pulling away from your shop, coffee cup in hand, it spilled, staining my suit. So a $1.50 cup of Mäni's coffee ended up costing me $7.50 at the dry cleaners. (Not to mention the chagrin of having to wear stained clothing to work all day!)

But as I said earlier, I figured that the problem was a mere oversight on your part, and would be quickly corrected. So I continued to stop at Mäni's each morning for my morning ritual of coffee and muffins. But, day after day, the problem continued -- each lid resulted in the same "accident." Clearly the lid was inferior!

So last week I complained about the leaky lids to your cashier. She told me that the old lids were no longer available and that new lid was all that you had to offer.

I *almost* reconciled myself to "making do," putting up with a certain amount of "spillage" daily.

But, this morning, not only did the coffee spill entirely down the front of my jacket, blouse and skirt, it also scalded my lower lip!

Now I am left with a decision: 1) I could change my morning ritual and get my coffee and muffin at Starbucks instead of Mäni's, or 2) change my suit to that of a heat resistant "bib," or 3) write to you and ask that you change those leaky lids!

I hope that you adopt the later. I'll miss those morning muffins breaks!

Sincerely,

Mrs. Indignity

P.S. I'm sure you're aware that McDonald's recently lost a *$6,000,000* legal battle to a woman who was burned by their "too hot" coffee. Please try to correct the problem: those leaky lids could cost you *a lot more* than a lost customer or two if someone gets seriously burned.

Was the request for better lids reasonable? Probably. Or was Mäni's more responsive to the reference to the McDonald's lawsuit?

We'll never know.

We do know, however, that Mäni's sent my wife a gift certificate for *free coffee for a month.* And they returned to using their *old* lids!

"Yes, We Have No Bananas"

Sometimes you just have to wonder.

A few years ago we spent the Fourth of July weekend at the Fairmont Hotel in San Jose, California. Our son was playing volleyball at the U.S. Junior National Championships, held that year in the San Jose convention center.

The letter tells the story…

```
Bruce Silverman
Mr. Indignity
```

Mr. Klaus Buchta
General Manager
The San Jose Fairmont Hotel

<u>Going Bananas!</u>

Dear Mr. Buchta:

My wife and I were guests during the Fourth of
July weekend at The Fairmont Hotel in San Jose.
(Our son was playing in the USAV Junior
Olympics.)

I am a (very) frequent traveler, and I have
always enjoyed my stays at Fairmont's
properties. Just last month, in fact, we spent
a delightful weekend at The Plaza in New York
City. So I have pretty high expectations
whenever I stay at a Fairmont property.

Unfortunately, two events really soured our
experience at your hotel. And we thought it
might be useful if we brought them to your
attention, if nothing else, to prevent a
reoccurrence in the future with other guests.

<u>Problem #1</u>: Like many guests, we arrived at
your hotel in a rental car, which we turned

over to the parking attendant. The volleyball
tournament schedule was such that we ended up
not using the car at all throughout the
weekend. So the first time we asked for the
car to be brought around was on Sunday
afternoon (July 7), just after we checked out.

Our son's team was playing for the gold medal
at 5 p.m. Rather than store our luggage with
the bellman, we decided that it would be
quicker and easier if we placed our bags in the
trunk of the rental car, which we'd leave in
your garage until after the game.

Unfortunately, the valet parking people were
not very cooperative.

They informed me that since we had checked out,
we would have to pay "by the half hour" to
leave the car in "their" lot. (The half-hour
rates are very steep!)

As it happened, another guest (also a
volleyball parent, it turned out) had the same
idea that I did. She told the person in the
parking office that the desk clerk had told her
that it would be "okay" to do exactly what I
was asking them to do -- without additional
charges.

The parking person than proceeded to *argue* with
the other guest, disputing what your desk clerk
had said. She noted that "the parking isn't
the same as the hotel, and that the hotel
doesn't speak for them."

I piped up at that comment, saying that one of
the reasons people stay at the Fairmont is to
NOT be treated shabbily.

The parking manager reiterated that "the parking lot is not part of the hotel" and walked off.

At that point I decided to simply load up the car and park it at the Convention Center.

Only the garage people then informed me that they couldn't get my rental car started!

So I went downstairs to see the problem with my own eyes. And what I saw was simple: the light switch was in the "ON" position.

I had spent $35.25 on parking (plus tips) -- never used the car -- and now it was "dead as a doornail."

Meanwhile, the clock was ticking. Five o'clock was approaching, and I was not about to miss the Championship Game. So I lugged my luggage back upstairs, checked the bags with the bellman, and headed back to the Convention Center.

Meanwhile, while I was dealing with the very unpleasant parking people, my wife encountered

Problem #2: Our son's volleyball team (which had also stayed at The Fairmont) had played four very tough matches that day. The schedule didn't even allow them a lunch break.

So my wife decided to bring them some bananas. (They are very rich in potassium; crucial for over-used muscles.)

She went to the Fountain Restaurant, which had bananas on display for their "signature Banana Split ice-cream sundae" and asked to buy some bananas. They refused to sell them to her.

She explained *why* she needed the bananas.

They still refused.

She offered to buy a dozen *banana splits* - the complete sundaes - "hold the ice cream, whipped cream, cherries and nuts" -- just let her have the bananas. No deal.

(???!!!???)

Again she explained who the bananas were for.

"Nope," said the manager.

Finally, he sold her *two* bananas. Twelve kids, two bananas. Oh, joy.

I know this all sounds pretty petty. But I think that hotels like The Fairmont have to live up to a "higher" level of guest expectation than places like Motel 6 or Holiday Inn.

<u>Parking attendants shouldn't argue with guests.</u>
<u>Restaurant employees should be smart enough to</u>
<u>find a way to help a guest who has made a</u>
<u>somewhat unusual -- though not impossible or</u>
<u>totally unreasonable -- request.</u>

We had really enjoyed our stay at the hotel. The room was delightful; we hung out a bit at the pool; room service was great. But since the two incidents I've described happened just as we were departing, instead of a positive experience, our memories of The Fairmont are less than great.

And, as I'm sure you know, that's about all it takes to lose a guest to a Four Seasons, a Ritz-Carlton or a Mandarin Oriental.

I'd appreciate hearing back from you about these two incidents. If nothing else, I think it would be appropriate for the hotel to refund the money we paid to have our car rendered undriveable.

Sincerely,

Mr. Buchta called me, and even sent me a nice letter as a follow-up. In it, he offered to credit my Visa account for the parking, and he acknowledged that the ice cream parlor manager should have used more initiative and sold us as many bananas as we needed. In fact, he reported that they were going to integrate my letter into their "guest training program."

No, no, no....

If my letter was going to become part of their training program, the least they could do was to come up with something to make up for the intransigent restaurant manager's refusal to sell us a dozen banana splits.

Another "Mr. Indignity" rule: elevate, elevate, elevate. There's nearly always someone higher up to write to.

Mr. Robert I. Small
President and Chief Executive Officer
The Fairmont Hotels

"Going Bananas – This Time to the Big Boss"

Dear Mr. Small:

This is a complaint letter.

In fact, it is the *second* complaint letter I
have written to Fairmont Hotels concerning a
four-night stay during the recent Fourth of
July weekend at your San Jose property. The
response I received from your General Manager
in San Jose, Mr. Buchta, was simply
unsatisfactory.

I think the best way for you to understand my
unhappiness with my stay at the Fairmont is to
read the original letter that I sent to Mr.
Buchta shortly after our stay. It's attached.

In addition to the problems outlined in that
letter, we also experienced the following other
difficulties at the property:

93

1. When we checked in, the hotel's computer was down. That must have created a great sense of anxiety for the front desk staff, because I can't remember a more surly "welcome" to a major hotel in America in the past year. (I probably spend sixty nights a year in hotels.)

   When we asked if our son had checked in yet, the clerk actually "snapped" at us, saying "I told you the computer was down!!!"

   When I told her that I was a member of your President's Club, but had forgotten my card, she told me that there was "nothing she could do about that."

2. Two days later, when I asked the concierge if there was any place nearby that sold high-speed photographic film, he suggested that I look in the Yellow Pages directory in our room. (I thought concierges are supposed to offer more help than that!?!)

3. On the evening before our departure, I happened to notice that the Concierge/President's Club person was at his station. I asked him to look up my membership information in the computer so we could get at least one day's worth of amenities. He said he would, and that he'd send our "greeting" up to us. It never arrived. Neither did an explanation.

Mr. Buchta responded to my letter with a phoned apology, which he followed-up with a letter and credit for the parking. (Though I doubt the credit will go through; the credit was issued in my name to my *wife's* American Express account, which we had used when we checked in. Her last name is different than mine, so it's likely Amex will be totally confused by the credit slip.)

Candidly, I think the hotel could *and should* have gone far beyond a $35.00 credit. Our inconvenience was major; the incident in the Fountain Restaurant was deplorable. The problems that I outlined here added to our frustration.

About four years ago I attended a cocktail party at the Ritz Carlton Hotel at Buckhead, in Atlanta. (I wasn't staying at the hotel.) At the party, a hors d'oeuvre slipped off its toothpick and stained my suit jacket. When I asked the bartender at the party for a bottle of club soda to use as a clean-up aid, he responded by asking me if I could go without my jacket for an hour. I said, "Yes," at which point he took the jacket away.

One hour later a bellman showed up with the jacket, which had been *dry-cleaned!!!* When I asked what I owed, his answer was, "sir, you are a <u>*guest*</u> at the Ritz Carlton."

That incident defines for me what great hotel service is all about. And since that time, I've probably spent $20,000 in stays at various Ritz properties.

Mr. Buchta, in his phone call, told me that my letter is now being used as a "training aid" at the hotel. I'm glad for that, but candidly, I would have thought that my inconvenience -- and future business -- was worth more than that to your company.

Sincerely,

Mr. Small proved to be a big man. He invited us to spend two nights "as their guest" at any Fairmont Hotel.

Things worked out perfectly in the end. The next big volleyball tournament was the California championships, held annually in January at the University of California in Berkeley. We arranged for a room at the beautiful Fairmont on Nob Hill in San Francisco, just across the bay from the Cal campus. We were given a spectacular suite on the top floor of the Fairmont Tower, with 180 degree views of the city and the bay.

But best of all, just after we checked in, there was a knock on the door. We opened it to find two bellmen carrying a *bushel basket* of – you got it – bananas!

We brought the bananas over to the tournament where our team's coach – well aware of the San Jose incident – actually fell off the bench laughing when we walked into the gym with our load of produce.

A "Mr. Indignity" tip: Most people allow bad things to happen without doing anything about it. They *settle*, and *don't* complain.

Complaint letters – good ones, anyway – are really an infrequent event for most companies.

So a well conceived and written complaint letter takes on extra meaning when it's received. And it's nearly always acted on.

FAILURES

As much as I'd like to say that every complaint letter I've ever written "worked," even I – "Mr. Indignity" -- can't claim a perfect record. In fact, I've received my share of form letters saying things like "Thank you for your constructive criticism." (Sure....) I've even had a few companies respond to my complaints (usually by phone) by saying something like, "yeah, you may have a point, but that's the way it goes."

(!!!)

But what really burns me is when a company doesn't respond at all.

It's rude. It's slothful. But most of all, it's bad business. For them.

The next two letters both failed to generate a response.

My thoughts on why they didn't work follow.

Bruce Silverman
Mr. Indignity

Mr. Peter C. Brown
Chairman of the Board, Chief Executive Officer
and President
AMC ENTERTAINMENT INC.

How to Frustrate a Customer.   (Two, actually.)

Dear Mr. Brown:

I'm writing to you – instead of to the
anonymous Post Office address in Atlanta for
"Concerns About Your Movie-Going Experience"
that's listed on your website – because the
story I'm about to relate is all about *flesh
and blood people.* Or the lack of the same.

My wife and I hoped to see *The Good Shepherd*
this past weekend at your Burbank 16
multiplex. Unfortunately, by the time we got
to the box office window the show had started
(our fault for being late… though the three-
deep line at the box office wasn't fun), so we
decided to see *Casino Royale* instead.

We stopped for popcorn and soda (the $10
special, which was served up by the single
slowest moving popcorn server in the Western
U.S.) and then walked down to the auditorium

where we encountered… NO EMPTY SEATS. Not
one! In fact, customers were actually sitting
on the stadium steps.

Very frustrated, we decided to go home. So we
went to "Guest Services" to exchange our
tickets.

When I asked the young man on duty how a
theater can be oversold (after all, you're not
in the airline business), his response was "A
lot of people sneak in." I asked why AMC
allowed that. His answer: "They don't care."

Not a good answer.

He didn't seem to care much either when I
asked for refund for the popcorn and soda.
(He said he couldn't do that.) In fact, he
didn't seem to care about anything other than
getting to the next person in line. The words,
"I'm sorry" (or, as someone speaking for your
company, the more appropriate "We're sorry")
never passed his lips.

We might as well have been dealing with an
automaton.

We certainly weren't dealing with anybody who
understood the concept of us being "guests."
Or even "customers." We were just a problem
to be solved… sort of like scraping your shoe
on the curb when you step in "it." Scrape and
move on.

This was the FIRST TIME we were trying your
AMC Burbank 16. So this was your chance to
win – or at least share – a couple of new
customers (who go to the movies nearly every
weekend).

I spent most of my adult life in marketing.
If I learned anything, it's that "Trial" is
everything… and you rarely get a second
chance.

Sincerely,

P.S. In this age of high gas prices, it's
hard to ignore the nearly $3 in gas we wasted
driving back and forth to your theater,
either.

Bruce Silverman
Mr. Indignity

Mr. James L. Nederlander
President
BROADWAY L/A/ -- THE NEDERLANDER ORGANIZATION

How to Lose a Patron

Dear Mr. Nederlander:

I ~~am~~ was a subscriber to Broadway/L.A.

I think you should know why Broadway/L.A. -
and the Pantages Theatre -- lost me as a
customer.

On March 1st, my wife and I drove down to the
Pantages to see "Dr. Doolittle." We got to
the theater about half an hour early. We
handed our tickets to the ticket-taker, who
scanned them and admitted us. The auditorium
wasn't open yet, so we hung out in the
fabulous lobby, enjoying a coffee and a
brownie. Once the auditorium opened, we handed
our tickets to an usher, who looked at them
and directed us to our seats in Orchestra Row
T. We sat down, chatted a bit, read the
Playbill, turned off our cell phones,
commented that there were a lot of empty

seats, and – as we have both done since childhood - began to anticipate that magic moment when the curtain would rise.

At 7:25 an usher asked to see our tickets; we handed them over – he looked at them – shrugged his shoulders – and gave them back. A couple of minutes passed.

At 7:27 a rather unpleasant young woman stepped into the empty row in front of us and asked to see our tickets. I handed them over; she looked at them, scowled and said, "Your tickets are for July 18th."

Since she had the tickets in her hand I couldn't dispute that… but I did say, "No they're not, they're for tonight. Besides, this show isn't playing here in July; it's playing here NOW." She scowled again and said that we would have to leave the theater.

It was now 7:28. The curtain was scheduled for 7:30. I told her that we were at the theater to see the show… not to leave; that we were Broadway/L.A. subscribers… that my name was "S-I-L-V-E-R-M-A-N, first name B-R-U-C-E," and that the show had been rescheduled and that I was certain that we were supposed to attend that night and use the tickets we had (regardless of the date on them). She insisted that we leave. I asked her how we could have gotten past the ticket-taker's scanner; she didn't respond. I asked for the tickets back; she wouldn't give them to me. Frankly, that made me that much more obstinate about not moving, so I asked to see the House Manager. She claimed to be the House Manager (though she would not tell me her name), and said that if we didn't get up to leave she would have to get "Officer Bobby."

I am a baby boomer from a not very good neighborhood in Brooklyn. "Officer Bobby" was not a threat to me. We sat.

Officer Bobby arrived. He ordered me to go the box office. It was now 7:29. I asked him if they were planning to hold the curtain until we got back. He smirked (I probably would have smirked as well, if I was him), said "no," and insisted that we leave the theater.

By now my wife was sinking very deeply into her seat. She was mad at me; I was mad at Bobby. People all around were staring at us… clearly, seeing us as troublemakers who snuck into the theater to steal the chance to see Tommy Tune sing "Talk to the Animals."

So, just as the house lights dimmed, we started up the aisle behind Officer Bobby and his friend, the alleged House Manager.

We exited just as the opening number began.

At the box office, we encountered – again – Officer Bobby, the alleged House Manager, and no fewer than three rather tough-looking (definitely scowling) ushers… who more or less formed a half circle around us (with arms crossed)… as I talked to the fellow in the box office. He checked the tickets and told me they were owned by somebody else. Quite mystified, I said that Broadway/LA must have sent me incorrect tickets. He looked me up… and said that we were supposed to have seen the show a week before. I said, no… we definitely were scheduled for March 1st.

Meanwhile, my wife was becoming more and more concerned about the (no joke) menacing crew of ushers, the alleged House Manager, who was shooting hateful looks at her, and Officer Bobby… all of whom seemed to be closing in, pressing us ever closer to the box office window. The alleged Manager suddenly reached out towards us (rather aggressively, I thought, since she had a very angry look on her face) – but it turned out that all she was doing was handing me a business card (of Raul Jauregui, with her name, Norma Borunda, Asst Mgr, handwritten on the back of it). The box office guy finally figured it all out: it seems that we had switched our tickets (which indeed were for the previous week) to March 1st (which explained the other subscriber's name)… and in fact, our "real" seats for March 1st were better than the seats we had been sitting in. The July 18th tickets were then handed back to me.

It suddenly occurred to me that I was the cause of all the confusion. We subscribe to the Ahmanson, the Taper, the Geffen, Reprise, the L.A. Phil, the L.A. Grand Opera, the Hollywood Bowl (and, of course, we used to subscribe to Broadway/L.A. as well)… and we buy ad hoc for many other shows… so we always have a LOT of theater tickets around the house. I keep track of them all by keeping them in individual ticket envelopes – with the event and night written on them – in a drawer in my desk. I must have somehow or other put the original July tickets for "Doolittle" in the wrong envelope when the show was rescheduled from summer to winter or after we rescheduled our night to March 1st.

Dumb me.

But…

We had missed the first 15 to 20 minutes of the show.

I was furious with the way we were treated by your staff. My wife was embarrassed; after all, we were publicly <u>thrown out</u> of your theater.

Worse, we were both physically intimidated by the half-circle of Nederlander Neanderthals who surrounded us at the box office.

All of which made for a dreadful… unhappy… humiliating… even frightening experience.

So much for "Talk to the Animals." All we wanted to do was leave… and not come back. "Joseph" could keep his "Amazing Dreamcoat." And I've always preferred tall (not "Little") women. I asked for a refund for the rest of the season; the box office person refused. I asked for a refund for "Doolittle." He refused again.

We went home. Very very angry.

The Pantages – which has been a part of our theater-going lives for many years – went from a place we always looked forward to visiting to a theater we never want to walk into again.

During the entire episode, not one person ever said the word, "please," (as in, "sir, can I <u>please</u> see your tickets"). Ms. Borunda never seemed to want to even smile. Officer Bobby played tough guy. Nobody thought to say to themselves, "the curtain is going up; it's easy to check out if this guy really is a subscriber – he just gave us his name – we shouldn't inconvenience him – he's even wearing a suit (!!!) and his shoes are shined – we could offer to reseat him a row up or a row down (many many empty seats) — we could offer to reseat the poor people who had the correct tickets for that night somewhere else (again, lots and lots of empty seats… many of which were good), it's a short show and the first number is a biggie, it wouldn't be right to make them miss it…"

Nope. It was "you must leave the theater."

I called Broadway/L.A. the following morning to relate the entire story and to ask for a refund for "Doolittle" as well as for the rest of the season. The lady we spoke to said that she would have to turn my request over to her supervisor, and that I would receive a call from her within an hour.

No call.

I called the next day and happened to reach the same person (who remembered me). She told me that she really couldn't say when I'd get a call from her supervisor. (Maybe <u>never?!?</u>)

I finally got a call earlier this week; a message was left saying that Broadway/L.A. would indeed issue the refund I requested. I suspect that I won't get the extra ten dollars I asked for to compensate me for the parking I really didn't benefit from. And I forgot to ask for a refund for the coffee and brownies, which — as you know are VERY pricey — which turned to bile as the evening progressed.

It would have been amazingly easy for someone at the Pantages to have handled this problem graciously, quickly and effectively. Instead, they made the problem my (the customer's) problem… they didn't seem to "get" that people go to the theater for pleasure, not pain… and they clearly didn't care that two pretty

respectable looking middle-aged people, who
they absolutely *knew* were season subscribers,
walked away angry at Broadway/L.A. and the
Pantages.

I actually do *not* subscribe to the belief that
the "customer is always right." We weren't
right; we had the wrong tickets. <u>But we could
have been handled right</u>… and instead of
becoming an ex-customer, I probably would have
taken the time to thank you for having
employees who made a problem a non-problem.

But I can't.

Because I'm now an <u>ex</u>-customer.

Sincerely,

P.S. Is Ms. Borunda *really* the Assistant
House Manager? If so, she needs training.
Smiling, saying "please," "thank you," "let me
solve this problem…," that sort of stuff.
Nothing too hard.

There are certain businesses that simply don't give a crap about their customers. The entertainment business appears to be at the head of that parade.

As you've read, my issues with AMC and Nederlander Theaters - Broadway/LA had nothing to do with the product they sell. I didn't complain about the movie or the show. My problem was with their badly-trained, rude, brain-dead employees.

Okay, I know that theater users aren't exactly the most highly paid people on the planet. I also recognize that they're rarely graduates of MIT or CalTech. And obviously, their employers aren't making much of an effort to elevate their performance.

But when a customer makes the sort of effort I made to complain about service, the company should at least acknowledge receipt of the letter... even if they're not inclined to do much about the issues that caused someone to write to them.

If nothing else, they should do it for defensive reasons. *People talk*... especially people who feel they've been messed with. I've shared my AMC and Broadway/LA stories with at least 25 friends... and I wasn't spouting words of praise. Mr. Nederlander and Mr. Brown both ought to learn a basic business reality: every customer you burn probably costs you ten more.

But I do have to admit that these letters violated my first rule: I didn't praise... even faintly. And I didn't give either company an "out" by asking them to do anything for me. In fact, I was pretty clear that I didn't want to do business with either of them ever again. So maybe the reason I didn't get a response was my own damned fault. Stupid me!

Lessons

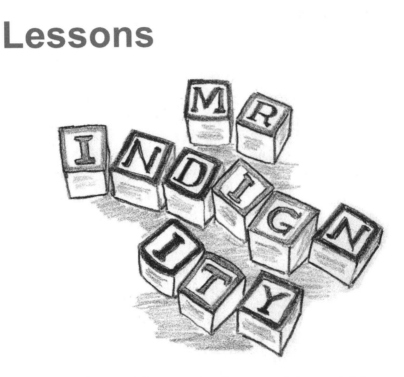

You've now learned the secrets of successful complaining:

1.

Write to the top dog. Worst case, his or her secretary will forward it to customer relations… but the odds of getting a response you'll appreciate will improve markedly if you take the time to figure out whom – not what – to write to.

2.

Demonstrate that you're not just some whiner; establish that you're a customer with expectations based on a pre-existing relationship.

3.

If you don't have a long-term relationship with the company, speak to their reputation, their advertising, recommendations from friends... ALWAYS find a way to say "you had high expectations from them."

4.

If you're writing to an airline, car rental company, hotel chain or any business that has a Customer Loyalty program (such as the American Airlines AAdvantage program, United Airlines Mileage Plus, Hilton HHonors®, Hertz Number One Club, etc.), make it a point to say that you're "in the club"... tell them how long you've been a member... and even how many miles (or points) you have. In any case, make it clear that you had a pre-existing "relationship" with the company... and that you'd like that relationship to go forward.

5.

Use charm.

6.

Use chutzpah. When in doubt, write!

7.

Be clear about what went wrong. Try not just to say what didn't work, or what they failed to do, but "how they let you down." Be dismayed by it. *Make it personal.*

8.

Don't be concerned if your letter takes up more than one or two pages. The length of the letter itself will send a signal that something happened that REALLY bugged you. The reader may skip ahead... but a *well-crafted* long letter is likely to be taken seriously. As direct-mail copywriters know, "the more you tell, the more you'll sell."

9.

If the issue has to do with customer service, tell them *who* messed up by name. Include dates, locations, times. The more specific information you can provide the better.

10.

If your complaint is about a product defect, state the problem clearly and be sure to explain why you simply didn't return it to the store where you bought it... or why the issue is something that goes beyond standard warranty protection.

11.

If appropriate, include illustrations or photos. Digital cameras, computers and scanners make it really easy to bring all sorts of things to life with a picture on the page. It also sends the signal that by taking the time to make the letter "extra" powerful that you really expect them to do something for you.

12.

Ask for the order. Tell them you want compensation, and what you want that compensation to be. (Use judgment; sometimes it's smart just to say "I want you to do something for me..."), leaving it to them to come up with something appropriate.

13.

Follow-up. If you don't get a response the first time you write, send a second letter (with a copy of the initial letter). If you don't get a response to the second letter, call them! Get a fax number or email address and send it to whoever you're talking to while you're on the phone with them! Don't let them off the hook.

14.

Gush! If your complaint letter elicits the kind of response you hoped for, write a thank you letter. It's the right thing to do... and, who knows, it may result in down-stream benefits as well!

I'm frequently asked if it's advantageous to write a letter on business letterhead stationary.

I for one have always written my complaint letters on my personal stationary.

Although I held very senior executive positions at a number of major companies (I was President, CEO and/or Chairman at every company I worked at from 1986 on), and my title might have impressed somebody, I've always shied away from connecting my employer to my personal issues. Unless you own the company you work at, it's truly inappropriate to use your business position to bolster your position in a personal dispute. In fact, in a worst-case scenario, it could even get you fired! (Stranger things have happened!)

You'll note that all of my complaint letters were actual letters... on paper, put in envelopes, stamped and mailed. Not emails. That's not an accident, or an indication that I'm technologically inept. Emails are great for day-to-day business correspondence and for keeping up with family and friends. But if you want your complaint to be taken seriously, it needs to stand out. Even if you could track down the email address of the individual you want to write to (which is often almost impossible to do), best case, your complaint will be one of the HUNDREDS of emails that person gets daily. It won't stand out. It won't be distinctive. It won't be personal. In other words, it won't work!

That's why it's tremendously important that your letter be prepared in a businesslike manner.

Your letter should be typed. Regardless of how clear your penmanship, hand-written letters are hard to read and don't seem important when they're received by a business.

It should be dated.

It needs to be addressed properly. Get the name of the person you're writing to, the spelling and title and salutation right.

If appropriate, it should be headlined.

Serif fonts (Times Roman, Century, etc.) are much easier to read than sans-serif faces like Arial or Tahoma. Make sure the margins are at least 1.25" in on all sides. Don't use a type-size smaller than 12 point.

Spell-check! And proof-read for sense. If your letter has errors, what business do you have complaining about somebody else not getting their stuff right? A complaint letter with typos and other grammatical errors is not likely to elicit a response.

The checklist on the next page will help you get started.

COMPLAINT LETTER CHECKLIST

Mr. Bert Boeckmann
President
GALPIN MOTORS, INC.

How to Lose a Customer
over $28.57

Dear Mr. Boeckmann:

Ten years ago, to celebrate my birthday, I leased a Jaguar XJS Convertible from the Terry York Jaguar dealership in Encino. A few weeks later the car needed something adjusted, so I called to make an appointment and learned that Terry York had lost its Jag franchise. When I asked where to go for service, we were directed to Galpin.

My first reaction to this news wasn't good. We live in xxxxxxxx, so it's a bit of a haul up to your location on Roscoe Blvd. Worse for me, I work on the west side… so service appointments were going to mean a long roundabout trip to work and back.

> ☑ *It never hurts to remind them of a fundamental weakness in their business that you "overlook."*

But I quickly discovered that your service operation was terrific. So, despite the inconvenience – and even though my office is just a couple of miles from Hornburg Jaguar's service operation on Olympic Boulevard -- I continued making the trip to Galpin.

> ☑ *PRAISE! Explain why you do business with them.*

> ☑ *Emphasize your loyalty.*

When the lease ended, I *bought* the car at Galpin. At that time I was told that I would receive a loaner car whenever I brought my car in for service at your facility. And that promise was kept… until this past Thursday (March 3rd).

> ☑ *Describe your expectation.*

When I told your service advisor that I needed a loaner, he said they "only give loaners for cars under warranty." I told him about the promise that Galpin had made to me eight

> ☑ *Lay out the problem… the reason you're writing.*

years earlier… and that they had always honored it. He told me that he'd "go to see the boss."

When he came back he said that "the boss" had offered to take 50% off the cost of the rental.

I accepted his offer… but not because I thought the offer was fair or generous. I simply wanted to get to work… get my car repaired… and then <u>never</u> make the trip out to Galpin again.

You see, I subscribe to the idea that <u>A Promise is a Promise</u>.

I also figure that as a TEN YEAR customer "the boss" might have been willing to take a few moments out of his day to personally talk to me.

The repairs to my car ended up costing $724.53. The car rental came to $57.13; my "half" was $28.57.

(I got charged the odd penny!)

I figure I've spent something in the neighborhood of $20,000 at Galpin servicing my car over the course of the past decade.

☑ *Sum it up; no more than two or three sentences.*

So, by refusing to honor a promise to gain $28.56, you lost a good and loyal customer. A customer who recommended many friends to your dealership. A customer who went out of his way for a decade to do business with you.

☑ *Tell them why it's in their interest to do something for you.*

You may recall that I originally acquired the car as a (birthday) present to myself ten years ago. It's time for a new car, and I'm leaning towards a Jag XJ8.

☑ *Show 'em you've got Chutzpah! Put them on their heels!*

But where will I buy it?

Sincerely,

[signature]

☑ *ASK FOR THE ORDER!*

P.S. It would be nice if you refunded the $28.57.

Mr. Boeckmann's son (who is now President of Galpin) called me. I got an apology, a check for $28.56 and a commitment to honor their original promise to provide me with a free loaner for as long as I brought my car in to them for repairs. He didn't come close to even suggesting that he'd give me a great deal on a new car.

He should have. When I finally buy that new Jag I'll likely get it from another dealer. He had his chance.

Good Complaining!

You've learned that more often than not, a good complaint letter will result in a great response. A *valuable* response.

But even I can't claim a perfect record.

- The IRS is oblivious to "praising with faint damn."

- My next door neighbor, whose tree fell and crushed my fence two years ago, still hasn't fixed it.

- The post office simply ignores complaint letters. (Actually, when I sent one to the local postmaster, he had the nerve to claim that he never received it… that "it must have been lost in the mail," which is pretty funny when you think about it.)

- Ex-wives disregard all complaints. It appears to be a law of nature.

Even so, it pays to complain.

Do it often.

Made in the USA
San Bernardino, CA
18 January 2013